WHERE'S THE GOLDEN EGG?

BILL HOPE

A Scholastic Book

Just before Easter, the most important day in the bunnies' calendar,
Tabatha Hopkins is summoned before the Great Easter Bunny.

'Tabatha!' he says in a great booming voice. 'Tragedy has befallen us! The wondrous
Golden Egg, which has the power to turn anything into chocolate, has disappeared!
Without it, there will be no chocolate for Easter!'

Tabatha, who much prefers carrots over chocolate, doesn't see what the big deal is,
but the Great Easter Bunny seems very upset.

'All the bunnies in the land are busy preparing for Easter. All except you.
Therefore, I task you with finding the Golden Egg before Easter is ruined!'

Can you find?

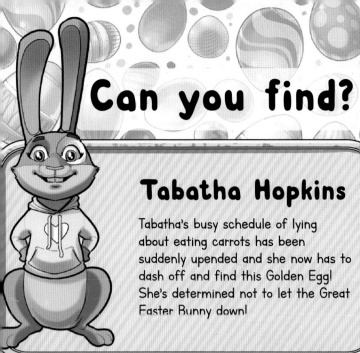

Tabatha Hopkins

Tabatha's busy schedule of lying about eating carrots has been suddenly upended and she now has to dash off and find this Golden Egg! She's determined not to let the Great Easter Bunny down!

Floopy

Floopy is Tabatha's cousin and just wants to play with her. But Tabatha has suddenly dashed off on some urgent errand! Surely *someone* will want to play with Floopy. Just look at her irresistible puppy-dog eyes!

@TimmyTweets735

@TimmyTweet735 is a big deal online. Timmy is dedicated to keeping his 23 million followers up-to-date with all the latest news on the Golden Egg disappearance. You'll find him dashing hither and thither, tweeting like crazy.

Professor Warren

Professor Warren is the cleverest bunny around. She's studying how chocolate effects the bounciness of children aged 6 to 10. There's got to be a connection! See if you can spot her conducting her research.

Naughty Ned

Ned is the naughtiest rabbit you've ever seen. He's had his eye on the Golden Egg for years and thinks this might be his opportunity to finally snatch it up! Keep and eye out for this bouncing burglar!

Bethany Bounce-a-lot

Bethany started hopping marathons to get a bit of exercise and now she can't stop! With the hottest new music blasting on her headphones, she sails through the world without a care.

Ed Hunks

Ed Hunks has been on a raw vegetable diet and he is pretty sure it's paying off. When he's not in the gym, you might catch Ed leaning against things and flexing. It's a tough job, but someone's got to do it!

Boris the Bunny Snatcher

Boris has never found any chocolate eggs at the Easter egg hunts and thinks this is very unfair. He wants a word with that rascally Easter Bunny. Boris will catch him if it's the last thing he does! Watch out!

DOWN THE RABBIT HOLE

Tabatha decides to start her search in the burrow. At the entrance, she runs into Bob the Farmer and asks if he has seen the Golden Egg. 'Oh, yes, I've seen a Golden Egg,' says Bob. 'It was heading in the direction of The Veggie Patch. But Boris the Bunny Snatcher is on the prowl. I had better show you the safest way. I just need to find my spade before we go. I must have it—it's harvest day!'

Can you find?

1× SPADE

2× OIL LAMPS

3× CATERPILLARS

4× BOOKS

5× GLOVES

6× MUGS

7× CUPCAKES

8× CICADAS

9× EASTER EGGS

10× ONIONS

THE VEGGIE PATCH

After finding his spade, a grateful Bob leads Tabatha safely to The Veggie Patch, where an epic veggie heist is in full swing! The gardener has completely lost control and the rabbits have taken over. A passing bunny on a tractor tells Tabatha he saw a flash of gold pass through the garden gate. It sounds like the missing Golden Egg! But the gate has been locked. Tabatha will need to find the key . . .

Can you find?

1× KEY

2× GRUBS

3× FROGS

4× MICE

5× BLUEBIRDS

6× SECATEURS

7× RED ROSES

8× TEAPOTS

9× GARDEN FORKS

10× BANANAS

the Medieval Fair

Tabatha bursts through the garden gate to find herself transported through time! Oh wait, it's the annual Medieval Fair! Rabbit families have come from all around to dress up and have a lovely day out. But Tabatha is here on a mission—she has to find the Golden Egg. A rabbit in a knight's helmet helps her out. 'A Golden Egg? Oh yes, I saw one riding the Ferris Wheel. You'll need a ticket, though.'

Can you find?

1× RIDE TICKET

2× LILIES

3× FAIRY FLOSS

4× PRINCESS HATS

5× DOVES

6× KITES

7× SHIELDS

8× FLIP-FLOPS

9× ICE-CREAM CONES

10× DRINK CUPS

ARTISINAL CARROTS

UP IN THE CLOUDS

Using her ticket, Tabatha rides the Ferris Wheel and hops off at the top to find herself in a fluffy white world up in the clouds!
She asks a cheerful chick in The Chicken Spa if she has seen the Golden Egg.
'A Golden Egg?' she clucks. 'I spotted one taking the Flying Stork Service back down to the ground. The stork can take you, too. He'll be tired from all that flying, so best take him a coffee.'

Can you find?

1× COFFEE CUP

2× POLAR BEARS

3× MAGPIES

4× HARPS

5× DRAGONFLIES

6× WHITE ROSES

7× BRIEFCASES

8× ICED BUNS

9× LOLLIPOPS

10× MILK BOTTLES

THE ARTIST'S STUDIO

The stork drops Tabatha off at a window of an enormous Artist's Studio! The studio is packed full of bunnies busy preparing for Easter tomorrow. Giant rabbits are being sculpted from chocolate, and Easter eggs of all sizes are being painted in every colour of the rainbow. Tabatha spies the Golden Egg making a run for it and gives chase. But in her haste, she knocks over a priceless sculpture! She'd better find some glue to fix it up before anyone notices!

Can you find?

1 ✗ GLUE TUBE

2 ✗ GLASS-COVERED ROSES

3 ✗ WORLD GLOBES

4 ✗ BUSTS

5 ✗ CUPS OF TEA

6 ✗ LAMPS

7 ✗ SPRAY PAINTS

8 ✗ CRAYONS

9 ✗ LADYBIRDS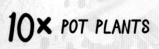

10 ✗ POT PLANTS

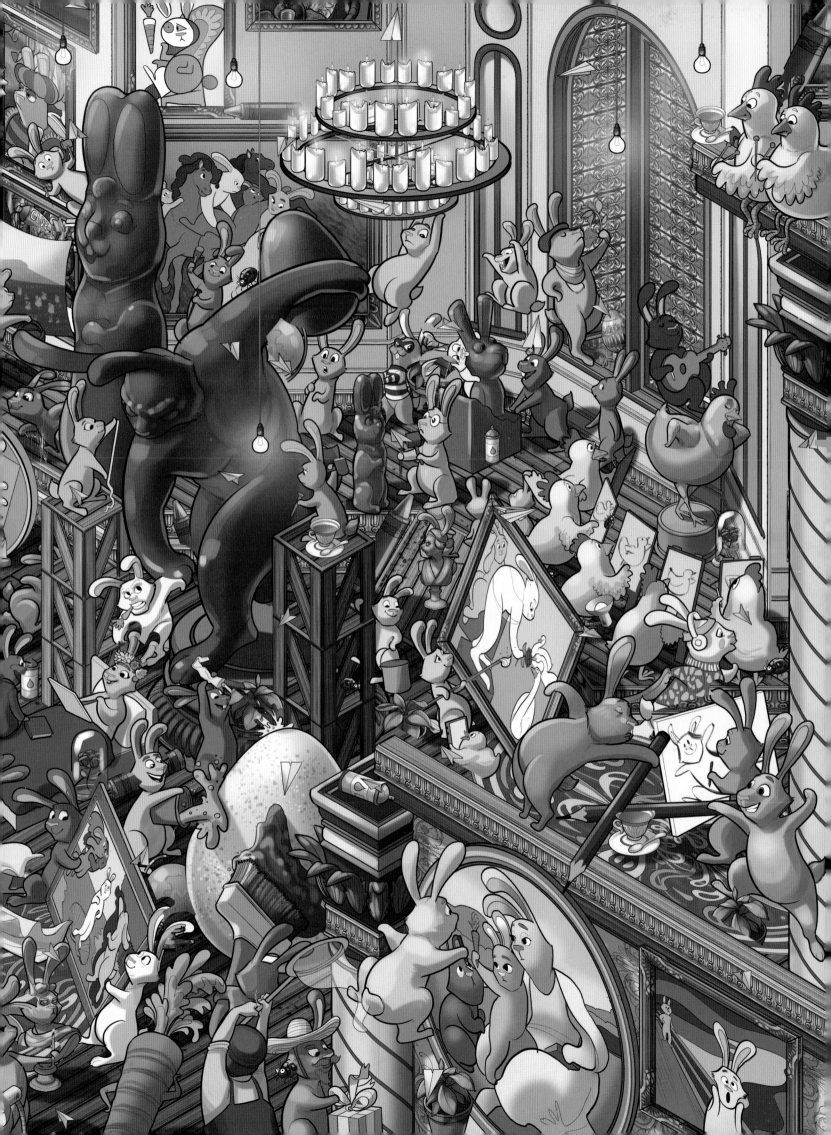

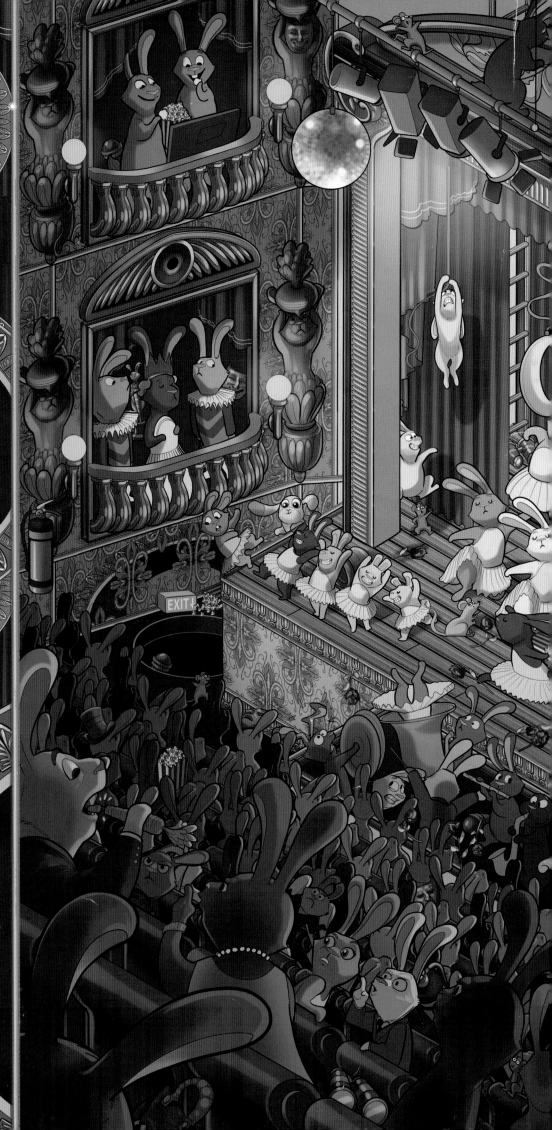

A MATINÉE AT THE THEATRE

With the sculpture fixed, Tabatha continues the chase into the Grand Theatre! A big performance is taking place, but there is trouble backstage. A fire has broken out! The Bunny Fire Brigade is hard at work trying to keep it under control, because the show must go on. In amongst the confusion, Tabatha sees the Golden Egg heading up into the rafters. She leaps into pursuit, but she'll need a backstage pass to get through!

Can you find?

1× BACKSTAGE PASS

2× TROPHIES

3× TORCHES

4× HANDBAGS

5× BINOCULARS

6× FIRE EXTINGUISHERS

7× TOP HATS

8× CHOC-TOP CONES

9× BOXES OF POPCORN

10× THEATRE MASKS

THE NURSERY

Tabatha uses the backstage pass and emerges into a world of colour and noise. While the grown-ups are watching a show at the theatre, their kids are being looked after in The Nursery! Tabatha just spots the Golden Egg as it slips away through a trapdoor. Unfortunately, a very upset baby narwhal throws a temper tantrum and blocks the trapdoor before she can follow. Tabatha needs to find a dummy to calm the baby narwhal down so she can get through.

Can you find?

1× DUMMY

2× PRAMS

3× PAIRS OF SOCKS

4× PACKETS OF CARROTS

5× BOOKS

6× BEANIES

7× RATTLES

8× BABY BOTTLES

9× LOLLIES

10× TEDDY BEARS

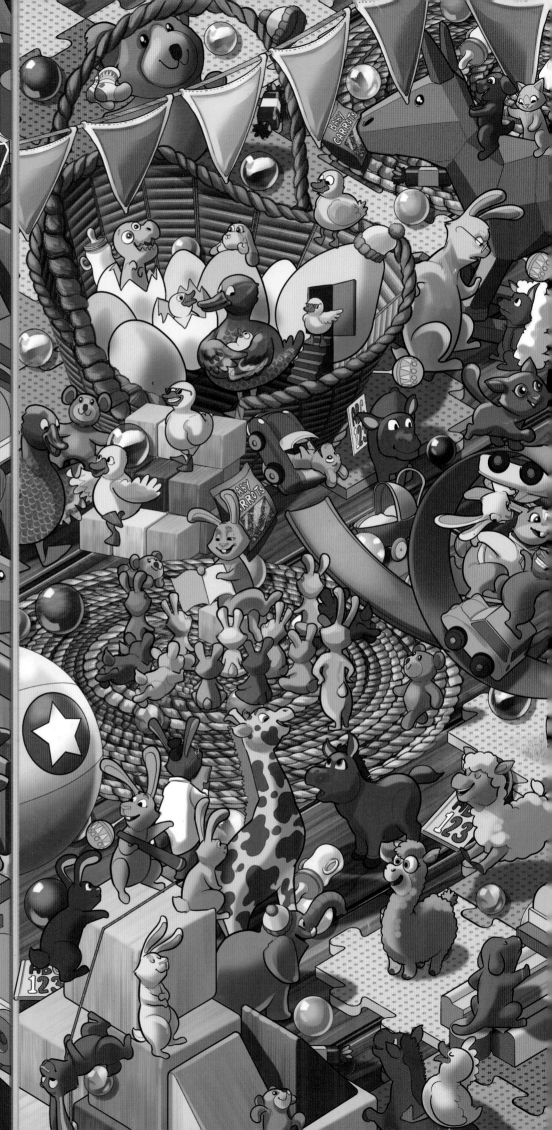

THE PALACE GARDENS

With a dummy found for the baby narwhal, Tabatha is able to escape from the cacophony and chaos of The Nursery into the bright sun of The Palace Gardens below. What sophisticated splendour! And what elegant bunnies taking a turn around the fountain! Tabatha sees the Golden Egg dash past King Louis the 35th and out of the gardens. But Tabatha can't pass the king without presenting him with a gift!

Can you find?

1× GOLDEN SCOOTER

2× ROLLERBLADES

3× UNICYCLES

4× PEACOCKS

5× WATERING CANS

6× VASES

7× WRENS

8× RED ROSES

9× BUTTERFLIES

10× SNAILS

THE EASTER HAT PARADE

King Louis was very pleased with his new royal scooter, and gave Tabatha leave to carry on with her quest. As she sprints out of the palace, she runs into a crowd of bunnies. It's a busy day at Bouncy Meadows Primary School! All the little bunnies are excited to show off their creations in The Easter Hat Parade, where the Great Easter Bunny himself will judge the best hat. This is Tabatha's last chance to find the Golden Egg in time to save Easter!

Can you find?

1 × GOLDEN EGG

2 × BICYCLES

3 × CAMERAS

4 × PROPELLER CAPS

5 × LUNCH BOXES

6 × GLUE STICKS

7 × FOOTBALLS

8 × CARTONS OF JUICE

9 × CRAYONS

10 × APPLES

After chasing the Golden Egg all through The Easter Hat Parade,
Tabatha finally scoops it up!

But what's this? The Golden Eggs wobbles . . . and jumps . . . then POP! Out jumps a
beautiful Golden Chick, who promptly changes her eggshell into chocolate!

'Hurrah!' cries the Great Easter Bunny. 'There will be enough chocolate
for everyone! Easter is saved!'

'Phew,' thought Tabatha, 'now I can kick back with a few carrots until next Easter!'